PRICKS

by Jade Byrne

For Jacob Love Jade

Published by Playdead Press 2020

© Jade Byrne 2020

Jade Byrne has asserted her rights under the Copyright,
Design and Patents Act, 1988, to be identified as the
author of this work.

A CIP catalogue record for this book is available from
the British Library.

ISBN 978-1-910067-88-8

Playdead Press
www.playdeadpress.com

PRICKS was first performed at Durham Gala, co-produced by Little Mighty on June 8th 2018 with the following team:

CAST
Jade / Young Jade | **Jade Byrne**

CREATIVE
Writer & Performer | **Jade Byrne**
Directors | **Ruth Mary Johnson & Annie Rigby**
Producer | **Jade Byrne at Blackbird Creative Arts**
Sound Designer | **Nick John Williams**
Set Designer | **Alison Ashton**
Movement Director | **Catherine Muckle**
Lighting Designer | **Tori Copeland**

With special thanks to;

Dick Bonham on behalf of LittleMighty, Caroline Pearce, Shannon Yee, Arts Council England, Christian Seedbed, JDRF UK, NovoNordisk Ltd, Dexcom UK & Ireland and Insulet International.

The above medical companies had no input into the content of the show, but have financially supported Pricks during parts of it's journey.

JADE BYRNE

I was born 16th September 1985 and diagnosed with Type 1 Diabetes 6th November 1989. I have always thought myself very lucky to have such a supportive and encouraging family around me; my Mum, Dad, Sister Amy, husband James and my children. I've never let Type 1 Diabetes stand in my way. I see it not as a barrier, but as a hurdle I have to leap over. It makes me strong, it makes me resilient. Although I have a very positive mindset most of the time, it is a relentless condition that can take it's toll on me mentally and I do have hard days as does everyone with autoimmune conditions. I studied Musical Theatre at SLP College, where I danced from 8am to 8pm most days and definitely had a few hypos but it didn't stop me from doing anything. It's there that I learned I had a real passion for acting. I graduated in 2008 with a top London agent under my belt. It took a while to secure my first professional job but in 2009 my professional career in acting began. I toured with Northern Stage Company as the original Claire in *Apples*, I also toured with Open Clasp Theatre Company. I've had a few great TV roles too in; *Casualty* (BBC 1), *Inspector George Gently* (BBC 1), *The Dumping Ground* (CBBC) and *Mount Pleasant* (Sky Living). I worked with Jabberwocky Market in Darlington, which was part of Battersea Arts Centre's Collaborative Touring Network and it was here that I was inspired to make my own show. After a glass of wine and hypo at Edinburgh Fringe 2015, Pricks was imagined and research started. After a chance encounter, I secured funding to begin Pricks' journey. I interviewed over 40 other Type 1's and parents of Type 1's as I really wanted to make everyone happy. I worked with artist Shannon Yee as a mentor to begin the writing process in June 2017. It wasn't until 2018 after a successful Arts Council England grant application that *Pricks* was created and first shown at Durham Gala Theatre. It went onto Pleasance Courtyard at Edinburgh Fringe 2018 and has toured extensively ever since. I continue everyday to be overwhelmed by the response to *Pricks*. I wanted to create something that educated everyone about Type 1 Diabetes but ultimately was very entertaining and I feel like I've achieved just that. I hope that people learn a lot from this show, and I ultimately hope that Type 1's connect with it, relate to it and enjoy it.

I'd like to dedicate this to my ever supportive husband, James, my 2 gorgeous girls and also in memory of my beautiful Mum, Susan Roberta Byrne, who lost her 4 month battle with Leukemia just before the 3rd tour of Pricks, but will forever be my most loyal supporter. I hope to keep making you proud Mum.
Love you forever, Jade XXXXX

CHARACTERS
JADE

YOUNG JADE

VOICE OVERS

DAD	Robin Byrne
MUM	Sue Byrne
JAMES	James Sloan
GIRL	Millie Harris
VOICES	Various
JAYDE	Jayde Connelly
DAVE	David Sturrock
ROSIE	Rosie Scudder

SCENE 1 | 12 PRICKS

(draw family on white board)

YOUNG JADE: I am like SuperTed, if SuperTed was a hiderer. I am the best hiderer in the world. They're not gonna find me. I don't want them to. They're gonna stick another needle in me. They want to inject me again with... inshulin I think they call it.

They think cos I'm 4 they can make me do things. Well they can't, cos I'm not gonna let them. Plus they're not gonna find me because behind this bin is the best hiding place. I've been here for like 2 hours now.

Yesterday they said I can't have chocolate anymore. Well I can if I'm low, but I don't know what low means, so I think I'm gonna start crawling everywhere, like this, cos then I'll be dead low and then I can have chocolate.

I think I might pop like a balloon. They've given me 12 pricks now, a human bean can't have that many pricks and not pop can they? They're gonna let all my air out.

My Daddy bought me the only diabetic Dennis the Menace toy in the whole entire world. I have to practice injecting on him. I have to inject him to keep him alive, just like they are to keep me alive.

Am I going to die?

It sounds like I am. They keep saying, die of betes. I don't know what betes is but I don't want to die of it.

Why am I broken? Can't they just fix me and it go back to normal?

They say I'm going to be like this forever. What if my forever isn't a very long time?

Will I ever see my friends again?

Will I ever go back to ballet?

Will I ever leave this hospital?

Will they ever even find me?

I don't want to die. I'll miss My Mummy, Daddy and my cats, Ally and Charlie. Oh and my sister Amy too I suppose.

I'm really poorly aren't I?

I think I'm going to die.

SCENE 2 | INTRO

JADE: I'm just testing my blood sugar.

Hello, I'm Jade, if you're wondering and that was me too 29 years ago or the 12 *(draw 12 on whiteboard)* pricks point as I like to call it, when my life changed forever and my parents life changed forever too.

This is a test strip, see, and I prick my finger with this, squeeze it to get the blood out, then I put the blood on the test strip like that and it sucks it up into the machine and this machine gives me my levels. They're my levels though so I'm only going to show them if they're good. (if high) Yeah you're not seeing that level.

I'm going to let you into a secret, I rarely have to do that now, because I have a Dexcom G6 or a Dex-a-com as my mum likes to call it. It's a continuous glucose monitor it's here on my tummy, so what that means is my phone always knows what my blood sugar is via bluetooth and it sets off an alarm when it's going the wrong way so I can deal with it, it's really clever, but I didn't have it when I wrote the show so let's all just pretend that I didn't tell you that.

So - this machine also controls my insulin pump via Bluetooth I've got the Omnipod Dash pump, here it is, I used to only ever where it on my legs but I'm being more experimental now and you can literally wear it anywhere. One nurse once suggested I put it in my cleavage. (*looks down at chest and shakes head*)

It took them 15 years to persuade me to get it. I didn't want something permanently attached to me but I'm an eater and I snack all the time and every time I ate carbs I had to inject so I was getting into double figures with my injections most days but with this, it means I only get stabbed once every 3 days so it kinda made sense in the end.

It does have the most annoying alarms though, so when the pump's about to expire this *(sound of pump alarm)* alarm goes off, but it goes off for hours and hours and hours until you actually have to change the pump. And if it malfunctions this *(malfunction alarm sound)* alarm goes off, and sometimes there's just no stopping it, you can follow all the instructions and it doesn't matter how many times you hit it with a damn hammer it just won't stop. The US military were once called out to one in a bin in a high school because they thought it was a bomb.

It really is very clever though. You can stop that now Sean *(stops malfunction alarm)*. So right now because I'm doing a show – and Adrenaline really affects blood sugar levels, it makes them go really high – so what I've managed to do with this is increase my background insulin whilst I'm doing the show, but don't worry I won't have a hypo whilst I'm on stage... or so I hope.

Welcome to Pricks. Pricks takes you on my journey of pricks, be that finger pricks, injections, cannula insertions or sometimes the other connotation of pricks. During the making of the show I met with loads of other Type 1 Diabetics like me and their stories made me feel like I didn't want to hide anymore so they're all here on stage with me, every prick on the way.

Let's begin.

SCENE 3 | MANY PRICKS 1

(each time Jade has said her line the sound cue comes straight in. Jade will accelerate with her responses throughout the scene)

JADE: I'm Type 1 diabetic

VOICE: Oh is that the bad diabetes?

JADE: I'm Type 1 diabetic

VOICE: Oh my Grandad's diabetic too.

JADE: I'm Type 1 Diabetic

VOICE: Did you used to be fat?

JADE: I'm Type 1 Diabetic

VOICE: Should you be eating that?

JADE: I'm Type 1 Diabetic

VOICE: Does that mean you've got too much sugar or not enough?

JADE: I'm Type 1 Diabetic

VOICE: Can I catch it off you?

JADE: I'm Type 1 Diabetic

VOICE: Did you eat too much sugar when you were younger?

JADE: I'm Type 1 Diabetic

VOICE: Oh I don't mind

JADE: I'm Type 1 Diabetic

VOICE: Well if you stop eating sugar you'll be alright.

JADE: I'm Type 1 Diabetic

VOICE: So can you have cake then?

JADE: I'm Type 1 Diabetic

VOICE: Is it true you're bankrupting our NHS?

(this is the last sound cue for this scene)

JADE: I'm Type 1 Diabetic not Type 2, and I can eat cake, a whole bloody cake if I want to, it's not advisable, but it's not 1989 anymore, we've moved on. It's nothing to do with sugar. I have a lifelong auto immune condition. I have a gene and when I was 4 years old I picked up a virus and that virus attacked my beta cells in my pancreas and it means that my pancreas can never produce insulin ever again. I didn't do anything wrong, my parents didn't do anything wrong, it's completely unpreventable. I was thirsty, I was weeing all the time, I was tired and I lost weight so my Mum took me to the doctors, my Dad thought she was mental taking me because I was weeing a lot, but she insisted I was tested for Type 1 Diabetes and here I am now, 34 years old, 30 years a Type 1 Diabetic.

SCENE 4 | 112 PRICKS

(change board to 112 Pricks)

YOUNG JADE: I know how Dennis the Menace feels because Dennis is Diabetic too like me. He feels like my mums pin cushion. You know what a pin cushion is? My mum's is a tortoise with a cushion on its back and she keeps all her pins stabbed in the cushion. Its back must really hurt.

They're giving me 2 injections a day now and pricking my finger up to 5 times a day and I don't like it. I don't like it at all, I hate it and Dennis hates it too. He told me so last night, when we were supposed to be going to sleep.

He said to me, "I want you to stop stabbing me and pricking me now," so I told him, "I have to do it to keep you alive". He said "I don't care." I said "if I don't do it you won't feel very well and you won't be able to play, and have fun." He screwed his face up like this *(Jade screws face up)* So I said "if you don't

14

have your injections then you're not going to ballet this week." He screwed his face up even more and told me to "shut up".

So then I just told him the truth, I said "if you don't have the injections then you won't be here cos you'll be dead."

That shut him up.

SCENE 5 | 1,112 PRICKS

(Change board to 1,112 pricks)

JADE:　　　　I've been told about my first ever hypo many times from my Mum and Dad.

I'd been diabetic about a year before I had a hypo. A hypo is an episode of low blood sugar when your blood sugar level drops below 3.9 and it needs to be above 5. You can't legally drive a car if your blood sugar is below 5, before every car journey you have to test your blood sugar and then you have to stop driving every 2 hours and test it again. They call it 5 to drive. Anyway, my first ever hypo...

My parents woke up in the middle of night to strange noises. Low, deep, gravelly sounds. Exorcist noises *(audio of exorcist noises starts to play)*. They ran to my bedroom to find someone had taken their little girl. Someone had taken her and replaced her with someone

15

that looked just like her but was completely alien in every other way. Their baby wasn't a baby anymore, she was a monster.

They tried to defeat the monster with Lucozade but it wasn't working very well so my Dad took the monster back to bed with him but after not very long he saw its' lips were turning blue, so he threw on a pullover and trousers and said "I haven't got time to wait for an ambulance I'm taking her to hospital myself". *(exorcist noises stop)*

On his way out the door he smacked its head off the door frame. The head was ok but still clearly the monster wasn't. He placed it down on the back seat of his car and then he put his foot down. Like really put his foot down. The normal 3 minute journey to hospital only took about 30 seconds.

Meanwhile, my mum got my sister up and got dressed and followed in her car.

They arrived at the hospital car park to find my dad's car there dumped with the doors wide open and the engine still running, just there for the taking.

The hospital eventually put the monster on a glucose drip... after 45 minutes. Once the glucose got into its system the monster slowly disappeared and morphed back into normal 5 year old me.

(blood testing sound – just the pop of the test strip tub opening, isolated though so it's obvious)

SCENE 6 | 2,112 PRICKS

(change board to 2,112 Pricks)

YOUNG JADE: I started doing my own injections today. Yeah I know what you're thinking, I'm only 5 but in 13 years I'll be an adult, cos 5 add 13 is 18. I'm dead clever aren't I?

My mum puts the insulin in the syringe for me and flicks out the air bubbles, but then I stab it in my leg and push down the plunger. I only like to do it in my legs. I don't like it anywhere else. It has to be my legs.

I test my own blood sugar too.

I do all that on my own. I put the test strip in, I load up the finger pricker and I prick my finger... Actually I don't do it all by myself, only cos the pricker really really really really really hurts and I like to bite a finger on this hand whilst that hand's getting pricked. Don't know why I do that. So my Mum pricks my finger for me.

But then I squeeze my finger to get the blood and put it on the strip and then I lick it. Not sure why I do that either. My mum calls me a vampire, but I don't know what a vampire is, they must like blood. I only like my own blood though, I wouldn't lick yours.

SCENE 7 | 6,112 PRICKS

(Add an arrow and labels it Dad, then changes board to say 6,112 Pricks)

(Exorcist noise starts to be played over the entire poem.)

DAD: Fast asleep,

Resting your head,

Across the landing,

There's a demon in bed.

You awake to that noise,

That only you know,

It's your little girl,

She's having a hypo.

The deep gravelly sound,

Of a monsters moan,

Absolutely possessed,

She groans and groans.

18

What to do first,

Get the drink or go hug her,

Focus and realise,

You really need sugar.

I must fix my baby,

I must fix her quick.

She's so terrified,

As she struggles and kicks.

Pinning her down,

Opening her lips,

Just pouring it in,

As she won't take a sip.

Cuddling tightly,

Stroking her cheek,

She's so small and fragile,

Tired and weak.

Her hot little body,

All damp with the sweat,

Totally floppy,

It's not working yet.

Some of the Lucozade,

Spills down her chin,

It's almost empty,

But some has gone in.

10 minutes wait,

Feels like forever,

As the colour returns,

To my delicate feather.

(blood testing sound – the pop of the test strip tub plus the loading and firing sound of the pricker, isolated again)

SCENE 8 | 10,112 PRICKS

(change board to 10112 pricks)

JADE: We have a wall in our garden. It was a weird wall. The wall juts out from the house and it holds the entire house up, but it's about 3 metres of wall, 3 metres of sloping wall.

Me and my best friend Katy are running around the wall, running around and around, Katy's trying to catch me but she can't catch me, she never ever can, I run down this side then round the back and then… That's it.

I wake up sat upright on a kitchen chair, in front of the cowboy doors, yes our house had cowboy doors this isn't a hypo hallucination it actually had cowboy doors. I wake up on this chair and I'm eating Rich Tea biscuits and Katy's sitting next to me and she's looking at me. But she's looking at me differently.

She looks scared. It's me she's scared of. I've scared... She's seen it, she's seen the monster. She won't want to be my best friend anymore. The monster has scared off my best friend.

I cuddled Dennis the Menace extra tightly that night.

(sound of test strip tube pop and finger pricker firing)

SCENE 9 | 15,112 PRICKS

(change board to 15,112 Pricks and add arrow to Amy and label it)

JADE: This is my sister Amy, Amy's a crier. She once cried at the age of 26 because she couldn't go shopping with me and my mum.

I also found out very recently that she cried because her husband ate a 2 fingered Kit Kat... the wrong way.

My sister had to write about who her hero was for her English homework. She wrote about me and I don't know why.

It's always been pretty shit for Amy in my opinion. Right before I was diagnosed I shared a bed with her at my Uncle Charlie's house. I must have wet the bed at least 10 times, moving to a different dry spot each time I did.

Amy ended up like the Isle of Man, surrounded by an Irish Sea of my piss, she's never once complained about that, she's never even mentioned it.

She told me she cried when I was 7, when they couldn't get a line into me in hospital when I had appendicitis. Actually, I didn't have appendicitis. I was just pretending.

I had a hypo at Amy's 14th Birthday tea in front of all of her friends, my cousin Belinda had to run into the restaurant kitchen to get chocolate, as back then they said chocolate was the best medicine for a hypo, they've now decided it's actually the worst, much to my disappointment.

I even had a hypo when Amy was shopping for her wedding dress. I clearly got sick of her being the centre of attention and wanted everyone to stare at me, slumped in a chair slurring my words and crying. It's a good look. My sister was my hero that day and she ran to the shop, in a wedding dress, to get me Lucozade.

Ok she wasn't wearing a wedding dress at the time, but it made my story so much better.

See this is what I do, I'm talking about me when I'm supposed to be talking about Amy.

I even had a hypo whilst I was writing this scene. I can't even write about her without trying to steal all the attention, which is what I feel I've always done. The bottom line is my sister is my hero and I'm an attention seeking monster.

(sound of test strip tube pop and finger pricker firing)

SCENE 10 | JAYDE WITH A Y'S HYPO, SHE'S HAD TONNES OF PRICKS

Dialogue from sound cue -

JAYDE: So when I was around 7 or 8 it was the first time I realised I was different and that there was something different about me. I was playing in my best friends Nanna's back garden and there was 2 of my friends there and me and she had like a swing set. I was getting really frustrated because I couldn't sit on the swing although I kept on trying, I just kept on missing the seat and then the next thing you know I open my eyes and I'm being carried by my best friends dad, and then the next thing you know I've opened my eyes my mums picking thorns out of my skin and she's crying. I'd hit the floor and rolled into a thorn bush and hypo'd in the thorn bush. So she's picking thorns out my skin and I turned round and I said to her, "please don't cry Mum" and it was then that I realised something was wrong, and the next day I went to the Nanna's house and I knocked on the door, to apologise. Now, what was I sorry for? And she opened the door and she said, "Don't you come back here until there's a cure" and I went home and I cried to my Mum, and I remember saying to my Mum, "I'm different".

(sound of exorcist then test strip tube pop plus firing of pricker isolated)

SCENE 11 | 20,112 PRICKS

(change board to 20,112 pricks)

YOUNG JADE: I'm in Year 9 at Hummersknott and I'm doing my SAT's. SAT's are really hard and today is my science SAT and I'm stood against the wall, in the corridor, outside the IT room in Trinity block where my exam is and everything's gone wrong.

2 years ago I started having hemiplegic migraines whenever I had a hypo. What happens is I go completely numb all down one side of my body, like even that side of my face

goes numb, which makes eating and drinking for the hypo all the more difficult.

Once my blood sugar goes up, then I get the worst headache on the opposite side of my head. It feels like someone's constantly trampling on my head and they're wearing football boots. Then the puking starts.

I can't eat TimeOut biscuits anymore. My mum once gave me one when I was recovering and I spewed it up all over the pink leather sofa.

My dad says "the sofas not pink, it's rose white". They're bloody pink like.

Anyway so it happened this morning, and this afternoon, well in about 10 minutes time, I've got my science SAT.

I look dreadful.

I feel horrendous.

I would rather die than be here.

What I need more than anything now, is to go to sleep and not have to think about frigging science.

(sound of exorcist groan, plus test strip tub, plus loading and firing of pricker plus pouring of Lucozade)

SCENE 12 | WHO?

(add arrow to mum)

(recording of my Mum reading poem)

MUM: It's not easy,
It never is.
A constant worry,
Getting myself in a tiz.
What will happen,
When I'm not there.
Who will look after her,
Who will care.

The worry is constant,
It never ever stops,
Like a song on repeat,
Off top of the pops.
You can't pause or stop it
Rewind or delete
It's always there playing
It repeats and repeats.

You imagine the worst
The most horrendously horrific.
The what if's and maybes,
Blocking out the specifics.
Will she be able to cope,
By herself at home?
Can she even have kids?
A family of her own.

Can she go off and study,

Have her own career?
Have the same opportunities,
As her friends and peers.
Can she mentally cope,
With all of the strains?
Will she deal with it all,
Without going insane?

If that's all OK,
And she does settle down.
Where will that be,
In my home town?
Who will be with her,
When I'm retired.
Who will love her like me,
When I'm no longer required?

(sound of exorcist groan, plus test strip tub, plus loading and firing of pricker plus pouring of Lucozade)

SCENE 13 | PARENTS

JADE: I know it's been really hard for my parents, I think it's even harder for parents of Type 1's today. Most kids these days wear pumps. There were no pumps in my day, but I think with all of these amazing advances in technology, actually comes a lot more management.

Parent's of Type 1's today have to test their kid's blood sugar at least 5 times a day, and they have to work out their insulin doses based on their insulin to carb ratio. What I mean by that is *(grab mini whiteboard and pen)*, every diabetic has different insulin to carb ratio and it's different at different times of the day. So for the most part of the day every 1 unit of insulin will battle 15 grams of carbohydrate *(draw 1:15 on white board)*. So if I eat a Wispa, which by the way is my favourite chocoate bar, that's 20g of carbs so I will need 1.33 units of insulin, recurring, to battle that 20g of carbs. *(draw 1.33:20 on board)*.

Basically you have to do a whole load of maths just to eat a Wispa.

Not only do Type 1 parent's have to do that, but they also have to get up in the middle of the night every single night to test their kid's blood sugar. They never get a complete night's sleep, like ever. It's like having a baby but for 18 plus years.

I put a post in the Omnipod Users facebook group, which is a worldwide group, asking for funny stories to lighten my day and I got 135 comments on it. Mainly off the overly tired parents of type 1's telling me the same kind of story about how they've woke up in the middle of the night to test their kids blood sugar and they've accidentally tested the wrong kid, the non-diabetic sibling, you should think yourself lucky Amy.

(sound of finger pricker)

SCENE 14 | 24,112 PRICKS

(change board to 24,112 Pricks pick up little whiteboard)

(sound of exorcist groan, plus test strip tub, plus loading and firing of pricker plus pouring of Lucozade)

YOUNG JADE: So I'm in Year 11 at school and the back page of my planner is basically plastered with this.

(show board saying Jade 4 Sloany, and then stick on whiteboard)

Sloany is James Sloan and he's in Year 10. I'm one of his house captains. They told us it was a draw between me and Anna Caygill but I'm not daft like, I know I didn't get as many votes as her, she's tanned, blonde and she's got boobs. Mrs Ord just thought I'd be better at the job, she's always had a soft spot for me. We live in her old house, the one with the weird wall.

Sloany doesn't have a clue that I fancy him. I always smile and say hi, but he has a girlfriend called Sally and let's face it, she's got boobs too.

I found out today that Mrs Ord has nominated me for a Positive Young People's

Award for all my work in the arts, like passing my Grade 8 ballet, despite dealing with Type 1 Diabetes. I get to go to an awards ceremony and they're going to talk about me on stage and everything and then I get to go up and get my award. I'm so excited. But get this, this is the best bit, it is soooo exciting. The Northern... Echo are doing a whole article on just me. They're sending a photographer to take my photo and everything. I think I'm finally going to be famous. I mean I was born to be, this is my time.

(change board to say 24,412 pricks)

(sound of pump alarm)

JADE: 2 months later, everyone's forgotten about my Positive Young People's Award, and all of the Sloany's in my planner are crossed out and replaced with *(draw on little whiteboard – Ben)* Ben. Ben's in Year 9, yeah I know it seems wrong me being year 11 and that, but he's completely gorgeous and everyone is talking about me again and I quite like it. I think I'm falling completely in love with him.

SCENE 15 | MANY PRICKS 3

(other voices recorded)

VOICE: What you doing that for?

JADE: I'm testing my blood sugar

VOICE: What you doing that for?

JADE: I'm about to have my lunch so I have to.

VOICE: What you doing that for?

JADE: I'm about to drive my car so I have to.

VOICE: What you doing that for?

JADE: I'm going to the gym so I have to.

VOICE: What you doing that for?

JADE: I feel a bit funny so I have to.

VOICE: What you doing that for?

JADE: I'm going to sleep so I have to.

VOICE: What you doing that for?

JADE: I've just woke up so I have to.

VOICE: What you doing that for?

JADE: I've been driving for 2 hours so I have to.

VOICE: What you doing that for?

JADE: I'm full of cold so I have to.

VOICE: What you doing that for?

JADE: Because if I don't I might die on you.

(sound of pump alarm)

SCENE 16 | 34,412 PRICKS | LIARS

(change board to 34,412 Pricks)

(sound of exorcist groan, plus test strip tub, plus loading and firing of pricker plus pouring of Lucozade, plus pump alarm)

JADE: I'm studying Musical Theatre at drama school, yes I'm a jazz hands kinda girl, and there's a girl in the year above that's, "become diabetic". I'm actually quite excited, I'm thinking I might not be on my own anymore, I ask her what type she is and she says she doesn't know, so I ask her are you on insulin injections or tablets and she really quickly responds with tablets. I then ask what blood tester they've given her. She says they haven't given her one.

You know what? She's actually pretending! That's karma for me pretending to have appendicitis at age 7.

I really want to say I know you're bloody lying. I wish it was you that has this absolutely relentless condition, this monster. I wish it was you that had to test your blood sugar before every dance class, every meal, first thing in the morning last thing at night, before every car journey, I wish it was you that had to inject every time you ate, before bed, when you wake up. I wish it was your body that decided to have a hypo mid class, mid routine, mid audition, I'd give anything for it to be you feeling confused, drained, hot, unable to move, unable to speak properly, so hungry you could eat the entire vending machine and still be hungry. I wish it was you that then felt embarrassed, mortified, absolutely damn right ashamed that you couldn't look after yourself properly. I wish it was you that now has to endure the hypo hangover, in singing, drama, ballet, jazz, musical theatre, anatomy, whatever!

But I don't, I don't wish it was you, I wouldn't wish it on anybody, I just wish it wasn't me.

(sound of pump alarm)

SCENE 17 | 37,412 PRICKS

(change board to 37,412 Pricks)

JADE: I'm in a night club in Darlington, it's called Escapades and I haven't been drinking, because I'm a skint student. Didn't want to miss out on the night out and the flirting and the fun but I couldn't afford to drink alcohol. I can feel my blood sugar's dropped. I'm really hot and confused and I know the bars closing but I go over anyway.

I know you're shutting and that but my blood sugars low, I'm diabetic, please can I have a red bull, I'll pay for it *(very slurred speech)*

GIRL:	Errrr no, you're just drunk.
JADE:	No I'm not, I'm having a hypo.
GIRL:	Errr no you're absolutely wrecked and the bar's closed.
JADE:	But I'm not, I'm having a hypo.
GIRL:	My boyfriend's diabetic and you shouldn't be drinking.
JADE:	Now that's not true, I can drink but I haven't been drinking.
GIRL:	You need to look after yourself better. I'm not serving you.
JADE:	But I'm having a hypo.

SCENE 18 | SEX STORY

(pick up Dave insulin bottle)

(Dialogue from audio)

DAVE:	So how I got diagnosed with Diabetes well, I was working for a big company at the time and I'd been on a course and I was driving my friend down there and she noticed that I'd been going to the toilet a lot, and I'd been drinking lots of water, which I'd also noticed over the previous few weeks and on the way back she said to me, do you think you might

be diabetic? And I, I dismissed it and I was like no I doubt very much that I'm diabetic.

Anyway it must have left a thought in my mind, I'd not long been broken up with my partner and I went out with my friend that night and we met 2 girls, 1 of which worked for me and we went back to my mates house and I ended up sleeping with this girl and afterwards I went into the bathroom and I was being violently sick, must've been the 4 or 5 lager shandies I'd had that caused that. Anyway I went back into the bedroom and she was like, Dave, Dave are you alright? And I was like no no, I don't think I'm well actually, she was like why what's wrong and I said, well, I think I might be diabetic, to which she replied, Dave you've just slept with me, am I going to get diabetes?

Needless to say I ensured she got home rather sharpish after that. The next morning I woke up on my living room floor having passed out after getting home, I went straight to the doctors to find that my blood sugar rather than being between 4 and 7, was actually 38. So I was immediately admitted to hospital and diagnosed with Type 1 Diabetes.

(sound of pump alarm)

SCENE 19 | MANY PRICKS 2

VOICE 1:   How come your blood sugars low?

JADE: It's that time of the month

VOICE 1:   How come your blood sugars low?

JADE: I think it's the heat

VOICE 1:   How come your blood sugars low?

JADE: I think it's cos of the excitement

VOICE 1:   How come your blood sugars low?

JADE: I think I miscalculated my lunch

VOICE 1:   How come your blood sugars low?

JADE: I think it's the antibiotics I'm taking

VOICE 1:   How come your blood sugars low?

JADE: I think I've lost weight

VOICE 1:   How come your blood sugars low?

JADE: I think it's cos he got me so angry

VOICE 1:   How come your blood sugars low?

JADE: I think the rooms too cold

VOICE 1:   How come your blood sugars low?

JADE: I think it's cos I'm hungover

VOICE 1:   How come your blood sugars low?

JADE: I DON'T BLOODY KNOW OK!

(sound of finger pricker and test strip tube pop)

SCENE 20 | 39,412 PRICKS

(change board to 39,137 pricks)

(sound of exorcist groan, plus test strip tub, plus loading and firing of pricker plus pouring of Lucozade)

JADE: It's the 8th of April 2007 and I've met a boy. Well I haven't only just met him, I've known him a few years. My sister is best friends with his sister. This boy is Sloany.

So 6 years after I've crossed his name out in my school planner, I'm at his sister's wedding, and I'm just chatting to my mum when I feel a tap on my right shoulder, I turn round and there's Sloany, looking very nervous, he says to me, "errr because I'm a groomsman I have to be one of the errr first people to get up to errr dance and I just wondered errr would you mind errr dancing with me please?" "OF COURSE I WILL!" I say probably a little bit too enthusiastically.

I turn to my mum gobsmacked at what had just happened and I say "I haven't even tried to pull him yet!"

I spend the entire night, obviously flirting with him, like I couldn't make it any more obvious if I tried but he really isn't picking up on any of my signals. I think if I grabbed him and snogged his face so hard it fell on the floor, he still wouldn't realise I fancy him. He doesn't even ask me for my number, but I'm not one to give up that easily, so I do some Facebook stalking and realise the numpty has his phone number on his Facebook profile.

So I text him.

My Dad always says shy bairns get nowt.

The text says, Hi it's Jade, I hope you don't mind but I found your number on Facebook. I just wanted to say I really really fancy you. Kiss kiss kiss. *(draw XXX on white board)*

(Move stool and sit on the ledge.)

And I waited for the reply.

SCENE 21 | 41,412 PRICKS

(change board to 41,412 pricks)

(draw smile on mum's face)

JADE: I come round and you're the first face I see, for 19 years you've been the first face I see afterwards. You defeat it, you slay my monster to bring me back. You are my guardian angel. Seeing your face when coming out of the unknown, it feels like safe. It feels like home. I never want your face to ever leave my life.

When it's not your face I see I feel mortified at the thought of someone else having to fight my monster. Pin her down, pour apple juice or Lucozade or whatever into her mouth. Someone having to restrain a monster the size of a 23 year old woman. What have I said? What have I done? Who has witnessed it? Answers I'll never find out off a stranger. I'm too embarrassed to ask and too exhausted to even bother.

I never want anybody to meet my monster she's like the wicked witch of the west or the girl out of the exorcist movie, groaning in a voice way too deep. I only want the people who know me as well as I know myself to meet her and if I had a choice, they would never meet her either.

But will I find someone who makes me feel like you do afterwards? Someone who makes me feel OK about it. Someone who doesn't care about my monster because they care more about me, like the way you do. Will anyone ever come close to being good enough, as good as you? Will I find myself another hero? Will I find myself another you?

(sound of pump alarm, turn off OHP)

SCENE 22 | BABIES

JADE: I grew up in a time where it was very much advised for Type 1's not to have babies of their own. I was told Type 1's rarely carried babies to full term, I'd spend most of my time in hospital, I'd have to have a C-Section because Type 1's babies were so large and I'd be really very unwell throughout and my baby most likely would end up in Intensive Care. A lot of this has now changed and today many Type 1's have lovely healthy babies without many complications.

Given that early advice, when all I did was play mummy's and daddy's, I'd already started thinking of alternative options and then my cousin Belinda decided to adopt and that was it. I'm going to adopt.

I want to adopt because I don't mind not giving birth to my own. Who really wants to go through child birth anyway? I want to adopt because I think every child deserves a safe home and I can provide that with tonnes of love and cuddles and kisses thrown in too. I want to adopt so I can give a child, or 2, the chances and experiences I had. I want to adopt because I think I'd be a great mum. I want to adopt because I can, so I will. I just need to find someone who is happy with adopting too.

(sound of exorcist groan, plus test strip tub, plus loading and firing of pricker plus pouring of Lucozade)

SCENE 23 | 45,412 PRICKS

(change board to 45,412 Pricks)

JADE: Today's date is the 4th of November 2009.

I'm sitting in Longsight Police Station in Manchester.

I've been placed in an office with a phone and a list of banks telephone numbers and I've been told to cancel as many of my cards as possible.

I've just been carjacked.

I was on my way to an audition and 2 men have threatened to kill me if I didn't get out of my car. They then proceeded to drag me from the car by my hair.

I don't care about the car.

I don't care about the bank cards.

I don't care about my phone.

I don't care about my laptop.

I don't care about my handbag.

They're just belongings they're long gone.

What I do care about is my injections and my blood tester.

They've stolen my lifeline. I cannot live without them. They can have everything else, but not that.

SCENE 24 | ROSIE'S DAD

(get insulin bottle named ROSIE).

REC 17 DICTAPHONE 1:53 – 2:42:

My Dad had a really bad hypo in the first day in his new, one of his new jobs. I remember being in a shopping centre car park with my mum and getting a call, one of the new people at my Dad's work this lady that he'd never met before just calling my Mum and saying "I don't want to worry you but Dave is lying on the floor with his shirt off and we have called an ambulance." (*laughs*) My Mum just being like "aw bloody hell" (laughs) because yeah he'd got really hot and they were trying to cool him down and get an ambulance to come, his first day in a new office, and I think the funny thing is, he'd sorta told them you know "I'm a type 1 Diabetic but I'm really controlled you know my sugars are really good" (*laughing*) cut to 8 hours later and it's like comatose on the floor and the ambulance is on its way, so that was a bit of a classic.

(sound of test strip tub)

SCENE 25 | DEATH

JADE: I've been googling Type 1 Diabetes in different areas of the country and I've come across so many local news articles... about Type 1's dying. An 18 year old footballer, a 19 year old student, an 18 year old survivor of a terrorist attack. Then I come across Emma Noble, a talented researcher at Newcastle University.

Emma was 4 when she was diagnosed like me, and she never let Diabetes stand in her way. Emma died age 46 from Diabetes complications without any warning.

If I die when I'm 46, I might never meet anyone. I might not have time to adopt. If I do, I'd never see my children grow up. I wouldn't be there for them like my Mum has always been there for me.

I'm sure I'll find them a great Dad but could he be the mum too? Could he sew? Could he braid hair? Could he embarrass them as much as I would?

I find myself googling sewing classes. Why am I doing that? I'm not going to die young. I look after myself. I monitor myself carefully. I'm a good diabetic, my consultant says so.

He likes seeing me. I'm not going to die young don't be ridiculous Jade. I really am very careful, most of the time.

I'm not going to die young.

I wonder if that's what Emma thought.

(sound of exorcist groan, plus test strip tub, plus loading and firing of pricker plus pouring of Lucozade)

SCENE 26 | 50,412 PRICKS

(Change board to 50,412 Pricks. Recording of James reading poem)

JAMES: She's away on tour,
It's 9am.
I'm calling to check in,
She was out late again.
She answers,
No, not she, it.
Her monster,
It's there, oh shit.

What do I do?
You need Lucozade,
Have you got some?
Jade, JADE?
What to do next?
Hang up the phone.
Call someone with her.
Balls, she's alone.

Right I'll have to do it,
I call 999.
Which service do you require?
Ambulance, I shout down the line.

I throw on some clothes,
Jump in the car,
Fly up the A1,
It's not that far.
What if's, panic, fear,
Thoughts flying through my head.
I need to get there now,
What if she's dead?

I cut the journey time in half,
Arrive at the scene.
Fly into a room,
Full of people I've never seen.
There's a look of confusion,
Then overwhelming relief.
She's OK, she's alive,
Good grief.

The paramedic fills me in,
He wasn't told she's diabetic.
There's 2 policemen there,
One is very apologetic.
He says he's sorry,
He thought she was on drugs.
He's never seen a monster before,
He's used to dealing with thugs.

It doesn't matter to me,
What's being said.
I'm just relieved she's alive,
And not dead.

(test strip tub pop, and finger pricker sound)

SCENE 27 | HYPO

JADE: I really want to make you feel what it's like to have a hypo. But when I have a hypo, I can barely remember anything but there is one hypo I'll never forget.

The 6 peach circles.

It's time to put your specs on.

(Jade put on specs) Now imagine it's 10 times hotter than it is now, 10 times more intense, 10 times just, worse in general.

(this next section is very fast and a little improvised but it always ends with the same 2 lines)

JADE: OK. Imagine there are 6 peach circles in front of you but they're dirty.

You polish the top left one and make it peach again and then you move onto the next and then the next but then you look up and see the top left one is dirty again so you go back to cleaning that one, then the another one you just made peach is getting grey muck on it again, so you polish that one, then the top left one is mucky again, so you go back to it, and then the other one is mucky again, so you do it again, then the top left one is mucky, so you clean it for a 4th time, they're just not staying clean, they just keep getting mucky again no matter how hard and fast you polish somebody keeps ruining it. Why do they keep doing that? You must get them all clean otherwise you'll die. You keep polishing tirelessly but as soon as you finish one the other is mucky again. You must get them all clean or the world will end. Someone is trying to open your mouth and make you drink but they're getting in the way, you hit them out of the way but they keep trying and they're stopping you from getting the peach circles clean and they're the most important peach circles in the world. And what is that noise? Get off my mouth. Let me get the circles clean. I'm trying to save you as well as the rest of the world. These circles have to be clean. They must be clean or we all die. Stop it. You're trying to kill me. I need to do this or we all die. Polishing polishing faster faster. Get out of my way. Get off me. If I don't do this we'll all die. I can't move, stop it, stop it, we're all going to die, we're all just going to die. You don't understand we will all frigging die if you don't let me clean the circles, GET OFF ME NOW! GET OFF ME NOW! GET OFF ME NOW!

SCENE 28 | 53,412 PRICKS

(change board to 53,412 Pricks)

JADE: You don't know what's just happened. What you do know is that your pyjamas are drenched and your bed is soaking wet, you've sweat the bed. Your hair, face and neck are all stuck up with Lucozade and you can hear the shower being run for you.

You feel like death warmed up a lot. You feel like a dying goldfish, floating around on their back in a really mucky fish tank. You've just lost another part of your life which you will never get back and will never remember, but your partner, parent, sibling friend, child, will probably never ever forget. A part of your life has just been stolen but then you've also been saved at the same time.

What might you have done, what might you have said? You don't know, but then they tell you.

You've accused them of trying to drown you in Lucozade. You've hit them, kicked them and screamed at them claiming they were force feeding you 21 bags of crisps, but they kept on going.

You're here, you're here because they were here for you. They were here for you and nothing else matters.

(sound of pump alarm)

SCENE 29 | 55,412 PRICKS

(Change board to say 55,412 Pricks and wipe off family except Dad and draw wedding scene).

Audio playing from wedding video, Father of the Bride speech.

DAD: ...and it proved what a lad of character he is, what a good sport he is and it just added to what I knew from 2 or 3 years ago. We all went on holiday together, I was still living in America and James asked me if I wanted to meet up with them in Florida and they were renting a villa, it's all paid for just come along and enjoy yourselves, so me and Heather and Charles and Harry flew down to Florida. You know, most of you know, probably all of you know, that Jade's been Diabetic since she was 4 years old and when she has a hypo and her blood sugar goes a bit low, it's scary right and I always worried what's gonna happen when she's older and me and Sue aren't around and it happened in Florida, I was laid in bed and I heard the noise that signals the transformation into the Wicked Witch of the West and I jumped out of bed and ran downstairs expecting to have to cope with getting her back in the land of living again, and James was already there with his arm around her, getting her to take the Lucozade, and I knew then, he was the lad for her (*applause*).

SCENE 30 | 70,412 PRICKS

(Sound cue to play immediately, Good Riddance by Green Day)

(Whiteboard drawing sequence – wipe off Dad, change to 70,412 Pricks, add drawing of girl labelled Mel followed by drawing of smaller girl labelled Meg, turn to face audience, quickly turn back and draw smile on Jade face. Then wipe off everything apart from Pricks and write

IN MEMORY OF MY MUM, 24/6/52 – 24/3/19

Fade to blackout)

END